MW01119127

Cows

by Robin Nelson

first step nonfiction

Lerner Publications Company · Minneapolis

What lives on a farm?

Cows live on a farm.

Cows are female.

A male is called a **bull**.

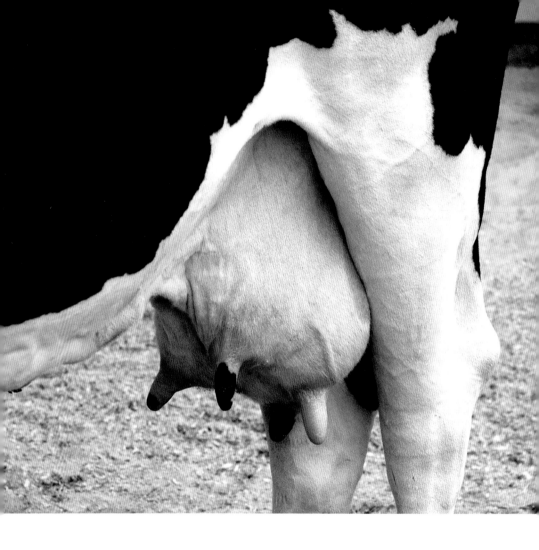

Cows have an **udder**.

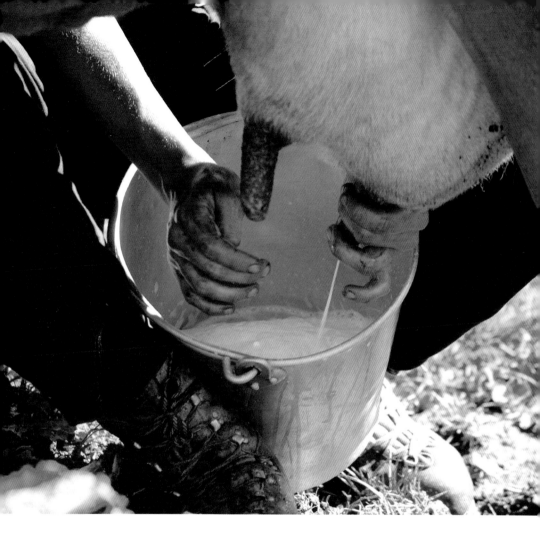

They have milk in their udders.

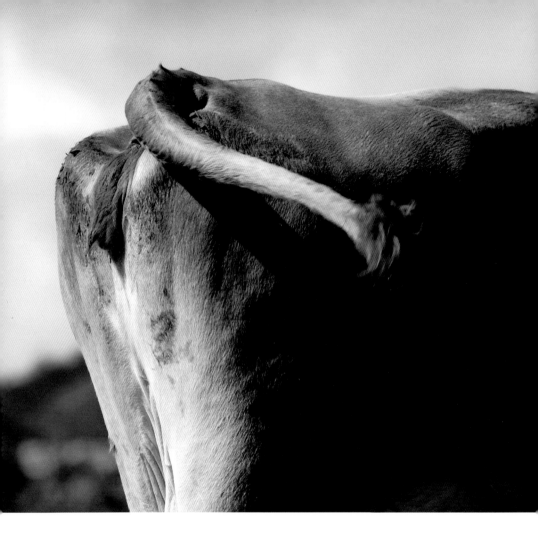

The end of a cow's tail is called a **switch**.

She uses her switch to shoo
away flies.

Cows eat grass, hay, and **grains**.

Cows drink a lot of water.

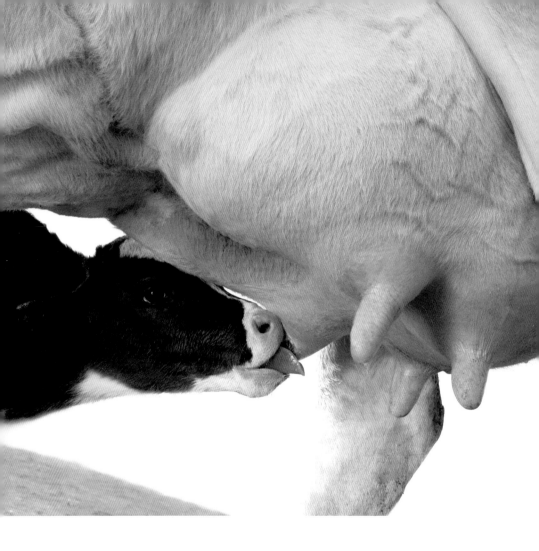

A baby cow drinks its
mother's milk.

A baby cow is called a
calf.

Farmers milk the cows.

Sometimes machines milk
the cows.

Cows give us milk to drink.

It is fun to see cows on
the farm!

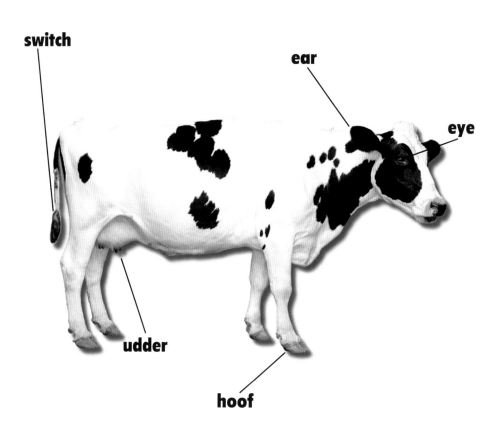

switch

ear

eye

udder

hoof

Parts of a Cow

There are many different kinds of cows. Cows can be many different colors—brown, black, and white.

Some cows have spots. No two cows have the same spots. Farmers use the spots to tell which cow is which.

Cow Facts

 Cows and bulls are also called cattle.

 A cow must have a calf to start making milk.

 Cows are milked every day. Sometimes they are milked twice a day!

 A cow can make 10 gallons of milk a day.

Milk is used to make many dairy foods like cheese, yogurt, and ice cream.

 Cows can weigh more than 1,000 pounds.

 Each day, cows drink enough water to fill a bathtub.

 One person can milk 6 cows in an hour. Machines can milk 100 cows in an hour.

Glossary

 bull – male cattle

 calf – a baby cow or bull

 grains – wheat, corn, and oat seeds

 switch – the end of a cow's tail

 udder – a bag of skin under a cow's belly that holds milk

Index

bull – 5, 20

calf – 13, 20

dairy foods – 21

grains – 10

machines – 15, 21

milk – 7, 12, 14, 15, 16, 20–21

switch – 8, 9, 18

udder – 6, 7, 18

The images in this book are used with the permission of: © Richard Price/Photographer's Choice/ Getty Images, p. 2; Agricultural Research Service, USDA, pp. 3, 4, 10, 22 (3rd from top); © ewanc - Fotolia.com, pp. 5, 22 (top); © Pat Canova/Alamy, pp. 6, 22 (bottom); © blickwinkel/Alamy, p. 7; © Biosphoto/Decante Frédéric/Peter Arnold, Inc., pp. 8, 22 (4th from top); © Biosphoto/ Thiriet Claudius/Peter Arnold, Inc., pp. 9, 12; © Wayne Hutchinson/Visuals Unlimited, Inc., p. 11; © Susinder/Dreamstime.com, pp. 13, 22 (2nd from top); © Tony Rath Photography/drr.net, p. 14; © Jim West/Alamy, p. 15; © Jose Manuel Gelpi Diaz/Dreamstime.com, p. 16; © iStockphoto.com/ bronswerk, p. 17; © Catherine Ledner/Stone/Getty Images, p. 18. Cover: © iStockphoto.com/Gregory Bergman.

Lerner Publications Company
A division of Lerner Publishing Group, Inc.
241 First Avenue North
Minneapolis, MN 55401 U.S.A.

Website address: www.lernerbooks.com

Library of Congress Cataloging-in-Publication Data

Nelson, Robin, 1971–
    Cows / by Robin Nelson.
        p.   cm. — (First step nonfiction. Farm animals)
    Includes index.
    ISBN 978–0–7613–4057–7 (lib. bdg. : alk. paper)
    1. Dairy cattle—Juvenile literature. 2. Cows—Juvenile literature. I. Title.
SF208.N45 2009
636.2—dc22   2008024737

Manufactured in the United States of America
3 – DP – 3/1/10